A Note from Kevin and ⎯

My wife and I often leave home with little more than a thermos of coffee and a direction. We may hurry to get to a place we've chosen for our latest project but once we arrive, our pace becomes slow and easy, car window down, arm on the sill

For more than 20 years, we've spent every free moment crisscrossing the Northwest, looking for treasures like those in the projects featured in this series of publications.

As a young man I spent many years drifting this USA, mostly the Northwest, but I have stories to tell about every corner. I was a good guy, but drugs and bad choices often landed me in bad situations. I've hidden from the cops in the great Dismal Swamp of North Carolina, hopped trains along the Great Lakes and walked dry creek runs of the Mojave Desert.

I didn't have anything: a few changes of clothes stuffed in a duffle bag but I always tried to carry a sketchbook and a set of pencils; later I carried a camera and a journal. As you can imagine, I've put together quite the collection of images and stories.

I walked along the Oregon Trail many times as a youngster, but not until I was almost twelve did I know those rutted paths were the trail. By the time I was a young adult, I already had walked almost every foot of the trail from Utah's Logan Canyon to Chief Joseph's Canyon of Washington State. That's why I know something is still undiscovered in that ancient trail—a lingering question that calls to adventurers, even to this day.

It must have been 1976, because Jimmy Carter had won the election, although he wasn't president yet. I found myself spending a little quality time in the tribal jail of the Northern Paiute trust lands in Owyhee, Nevada. I had been invited to relax for a few days as their guest while they decided if I really was just passing through as I claimed, or if I had been involved in a recent theft of gold-laden slag from local mines (remind me to tell you that story).

The night-shift jail keeper was an ancient man. I never asked his age, but he had to be every bit of ninety and could easily have been a hundred or older.

I was the jail's only guest. Probably because the old man was bored, or maybe because he was lonely, he and I had conversations well into the night, and he often sat with me at breakfast, just outside the unlocked cell door. The old jailer told wonderful, rambling stories about the trail he called, "The Great Medicine Road," or sometimes, "The Way Through." His stories often started with a legend of great leaders and ended with lost battles and loved ones.

The time I spent in that small drunk-tank served as a keystone event in my life. It opened my mind to cultures and religions of other people, quelled prejudices seeded in my childhood, and established a relationship with the people and places that make up the history of that grand Oregon Trail.

The whole of the Oregon Trail was a battlefield, every foot. From the eastern slopes of the Laramie Mountains in Wyoming to the western slopes of Oregon's Blue Mountains, pioneers   endured unbelievable tribulations. They traveled with the hope of a better future for their children, but as they came, they destroyed ancient, indigenous cultures and voided the dreams of the native families of this land.

A single publication can show only a glimpse, but I hope it conveys the heart of my work. I'm not afraid to vaunt an amazing collection of representational images focused on the historic buildings scattered along the Oregon Trail.

Uncounted hours have been spent cataloging these vanishing Northwest treasures. I've dedicated my life to this project:, over 500,000 miles driven on back-roads and byways, endless hours of artwork, many gallons of cold coffee and hundreds of soggy sandwiches have gone into the creation of this collection, and I am using the pages in this series of publications to show you some of that work.

Many of the old buildings I've pictured are already gone with many more collapsing or being demolished every day. Not all the pictures found in these publications are beautiful, but each one has a story behind it. I try to help tell that story, and maybe add a little color.

"On Bear Lake," Bear River Project

Many of the stories and histories came to me secondhand, as I gathered them during visits with local folks. While the accuracy of such materials cannot be guaranteed, reputable resources were consulted to check facts. All the artists, artisans, and historical personalities featured here are real, but other characters are fictitious, and any resemblance to real persons, living or dead, is purely coincidental.

The Camas Project
by ckevinswan

There is a prairie land that runs like a belt across the midsection of Idaho; a natural divide between the high desert of the Snake River plains and the stunning scenery of Idaho's mountain lands.

A geographer would probably disagree with me about where it starts and ends but from a drifter's point of view, it starts on the western slopes of the Grand Tetons, south near Victor, Idaho then plays north of the Island Park Reservoir. The prairie then meanders through the belly of the mountain lands, falls into Hells Canyon, then continues west to the Blue Mountains of Oregon.

That prairie has inspired many of my wanderings and been the heart of many projects. This publication features a small part of the Camas Project, from Mountain Home to just a few miles east of Fairfield, Idaho at Willow Creek.

An early Sears and Roebuck kit home delivered by freight wagon, $725.00

The mountain front pictured above is the Soldier Mountains. The snow-covered summit to the far left is Smoky Dome. At 10,095 feet, it is the highest peak of the Soldier Range.

Smoky Dome rises about 5,000 feet over the Camas Prairie and stood witness to early frontiersman, travelers of the Oregon Trail, the burgeoning of Anglo American settlements and some of the most ferocious fighting of the Bannock War.

Views from the summit encompass the Pioneer, Smoky, and Trinity Mountains as well as the Bennett Hills, homeland of many Bannock families.

A few miles north of Mountain Home on Highway 20 is a historical marker for Rattle Snake Stage Stop and the original site of Mountain Home. Travelers of the Oregon Tail could continue west from here or go north and follow the hope of land newly opened for settlers, the land of Camas Prairie and the Wood River Valley.

The first place of interest is Tollgate, Idaho. It isn't much more than a historical marker now but I once spent most of a day in an odd little café/convenience store drinking coffee, waiting out an October storm and hoping to hitch a ride through the Wood River Valley.

Heavy equipment wagons had to avoid the steep Syrup Creek grade on Goodale's Cutoff of the Oregon Trail until James Porter established a toll road allowing access to the gold mines and spring-up towns like Rocky Bar, Idaho.

John's dugout site.

John "Behind-the-Rocks" McKeown lived in a dugout along the toll road, about halfway between Prairie and the Toll Gate Stop.

He made his living as a mule skinner, piloting the heavy freight wagons up and down the steep grades to the mining camps and tending to animals of freighters who would stop to rest their horses.

The legend is that John never removed his clothing or bathed. John passed away in 1915, in a Mountain Home hospital. Because of the overwhelming smell, the hospital staff gave him a bath. While undressing him, they counted at least seven layers of clothing in various stages of decay. As the legend goes, that bath led to his demise.

A few relics still remain of Rocky Bar, ID

Farmstead near Prairie, Idaho

Near Featherville, Idaho

"County Line School"

East of Toll Gate , as you near Hill City, turn south at Schoolhouse Road. There you will find access roads into the Centennial Marsh.

At a little over 5000 feet above sea level, semi-bowled land creates a large floodplain for Camas Creek.

"White Camas"

The Camas Prairie has always been rich in deep, volcanic soil and the Bannock families that dwelt in this land wanted for nothing, but the starchy, staple food of the prairies has a dark secret. Its brother, the White Camas, isn't as benign as the blue-flowered cousin used as a food source.

An old man of the Nez Perce (Nimmiipuu) people once told me his wife was a healer and knew medicinal recipes for White Camas root. "If you take just a little it is good, it brings energy and vigor." He smiled. "I kept my wives happy with the vision potion." He laughed quietly, almost to himself. "A little more and it brings visions." He looked deep into my eyes, still smiling. "Some people have visions of gods, others are not so lucky." He pushed a little lump of the plant's root into his mouth. "A little more brings madness and still a little bit more, it brings death."

Spring in the
Centennial Marsh.

     Spring on the marshlands of the Camas Prairie was a celebrated time of plenty for the Bannock families that inhabited the land. Fishing and birding supplied important meat at the end of long, cold winters. Deer, elk and buffalo came to the wetlands following the marsh grasses of early spring . Camas root, though harvested most of the year was sweeter, softer and easier to dig. The people lived in extended family lodges in family groups with no appointed leaders but did have a communal leader who served as a director of ceremonies, dances, festivals and hunts.

     Pioneers avoided the marsh lands. Sticky mud weighed down wagon wheels and the soft, wet dirt opened to sinkholes with little warning, killing ox and horse and braking axles. Goodale's Cut Off followed the base of the Soldier Mountains north of the wetlands.

Images of the Camas Prairie

Cabin on Camas Series # 3 of 4

Local settlers allowed their hogs to feed on the camas root, and the cavalry of Fort Boise grazed their livestock on the Camas Prairie in the area of Hill City and Corral, eating the flowering camas plant and adding to the depletion of the Bannocks traditional food source. In 1869, a treaty was ratified by the US Senate that provided trust lands of the "Kansas Prairie" to the local Bannock people. A little problem: there is no Kansas Prairie in Idaho and because of that mistake (purposeful?) the treaty wasn't honored and the rights of the Bannock families were ignored. Their leaders objected to no avail. This all led to the Bannock War of 1878.

Chief Buffalo Horn directed a large contingent of Bannock, Shoshone and Paiute warriors in a hit-and-run war effort against the US Army along the Snake River and on Camas Prairie. At one time Chief Buffalo Horn served as a Scout for the United States Army under General George Custer. He was badly wounded in June of 1878 and after several days travel, he asked to be left behind to die

Seems like a thousand years ago. I was working for a dairy in Twin Falls, Idaho. My boss ordered a load of hay from a farmer near Hill City and he sent me with the truck driver to get the load. We stopped at the old stage stop then doing business as a bar and grill in Corral just as a buster of a windstorm came hard on the Camas Prairie.

As it is with large trucks, ours was ordered off the road until the storm passed. From what I heard on the radio the layover would last until late that night if not early the next morning, so the driver and I settled in at a table of the bar and grill to make the best of it.

A few hours into an afternoon spent listening to Hank Williams, Jr. and Ray Price, a couple of locals came in to collect an order they had placed sometime earlier. Wasn't any trick to figure these folks were on their way to a party and were already celebrating the event.

The owner of the bar approached the driver and me. "Sorry, boys, I'm gonna close up here in a little." He hurried to bus our table as he talked. "I know you fellas got nowhere to go, so I'm working on getting you an invitation to a birthday party."

Turned out we were welcome at the party. We joined the bar owner in his pick-up and were on our way. I don't remember the name of the old fella whose birthday it was, but I do remember passing a sign as we turned to the house that read, "Field's Tree Farm." Many cars and trucks were already there, a nice-sized crowd of folks were fighting a heavy wind as they stood around a smoking half-barrel with a big side of beef sizzling away and filling the barnyard with smoke and wonderful smells. Some folks were already cutting slices for a taste, and I was anxious for a sample myself.

It was a great night: the wind finally blew itself down to a small breeze and didn't dampen the fun of the party or the spirit of the Camas people even a little bit. They had fought a piano into the barn, there were guitars and fiddles, a banjo, and a big fella wearing bib overalls played the spoons and a washboard. Mostly country music, some stepped-up gospel and even a smattering of rockabilly music, a little dancing, lots of barbeque, tater salad, home baked beans and corn on the cob. I had a great time and met lots of wonderful people.

The old stage stop/bar and grill is closed now and the last time I saw, the old barn at the tree farm had been replaced with a nice new steel building.

It was that first visit to the Camas Prairie that planted the seed to create these publications.

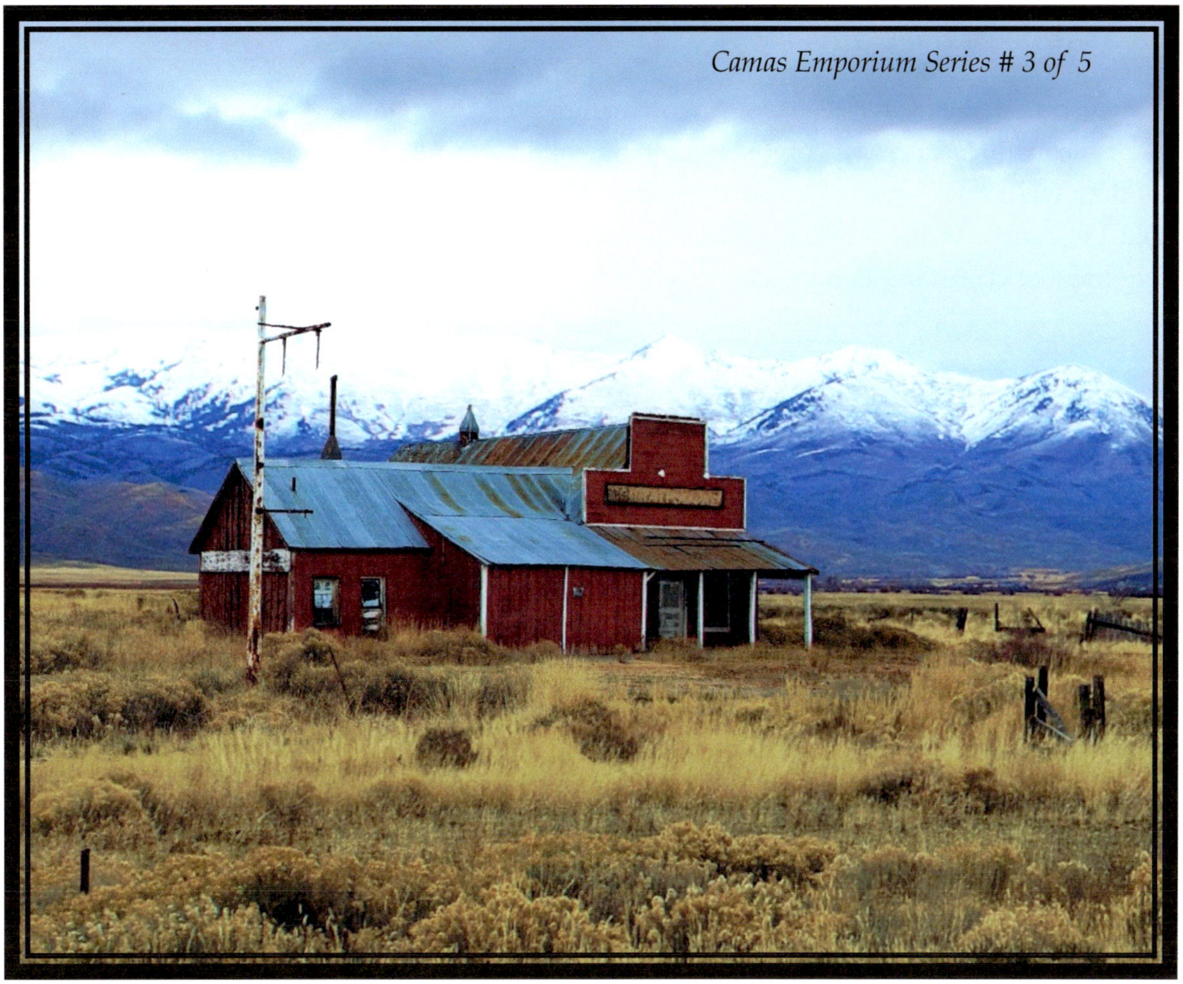
Camas Emporium Series # 3 of 5

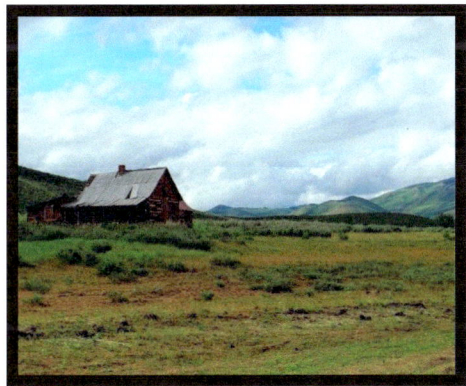

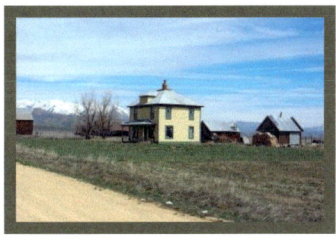

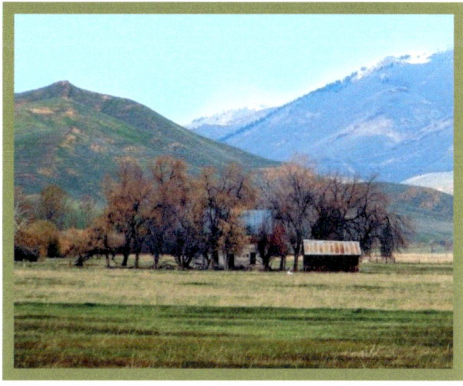

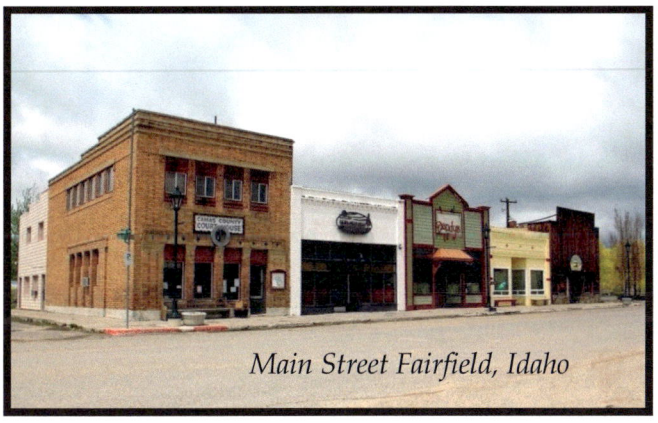

Main Street Fairfield, Idaho

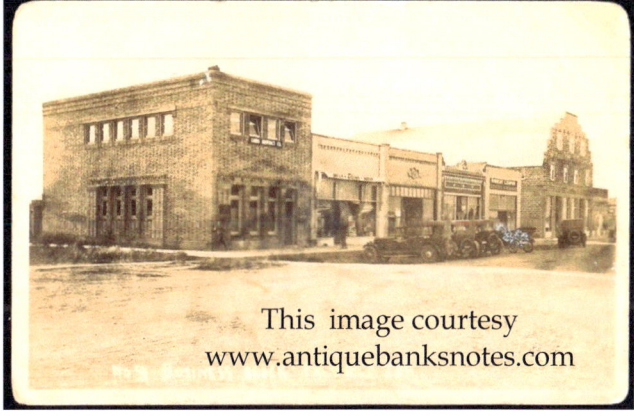

This image courtesy
www.antiquebanksnotes.com

Native People of the Camas

They called themselves *Pah'anuck*, which translates to "Bannock" (From across the Water). They're also called *Numa* (The People). Neighbors called them *Ba-naite* (The People from Below). In general, they were taller and lighter-skinned than the Northern Piaute and Shoshone people. I was once told the source of the word Bannock was a combination of Paiute words, "bamb" (hair) and "nack" (going back) creating Bampnack.

The Bannock lived a hunter-gatherer lifestyle even into the early 1900s

Bannock men wore war shirts of two deer skins, breechclouts, leggings and moccasins during warfare and painted their faces with colorful war paint. Leggings were worn from the hip to the ankle.

Women wore dresses, skirts, leggings and moccasins made of deer and elk skins and they wore decorations of deer hooves, bird bones and things like rabbit toe earrings and clam shells that had been bartered from costal people at powwows and council meetings. They often adorned themselves with tattoos and body piercings like ear and lip plugs.

By the late 1800s Bannock dress was a mix of contemporary Anglo American and traditional fabrics and clothing

The Bannock called Southeastern Oregon and all of Southern Idaho home but were equally comfortable in Montana, Nevada, and Wyoming. It wasn't a bit unusual for them to make buffalo hunting trips following the legendary Bannock Trail through the area now known as Yellowstone Park and as far north as Canada. Lower elevations of the Camas Prairie were favorite wintering havens for them and their close relatives, the Shoshone and Northern Paiute.

Mostly hunters and gatherers, they moved with the seasons, making use of the rich resources of the grasslands, and were often referred to as *de-de-veewah* (travelers).

Many of Idaho's native people called themselves by the foods they ate: *Agaideka* (Salmon-eaters), *Tuku-deka* (Sheep-eaters), *Kuchun-deka* (Buffalo-eaters), *Kamu-deka* (Rabbit-eaters), *Hukan-deka* (Seed-eaters), *Deheya'a-deka* (Deer-eaters), *Yamba-deka* (Root-eaters), and the list goes on. The Shoshone of Idaho are the most northerly of the Uto-Aztecan speaking people and share similar lifestyle, traditions and beliefs as the Bannock. The Comanche, Hopi, and Ute also share their language heritage.

Today, descendants of the Lemhi, Boise Valley, Bruneau, Weiser and other bands of Shoshone and Bannock reside on the trust lands of Fort Hall, Idaho but return to their traditional lands to hunt, socialize, and practice their traditions and ceremonies.

In 1832, Nathaniel Wyeth organized the expedition that established a trading post that in 1834 became Fort Hall. A legend is told that as Wyeth traveled, he shot a buffalo and where it fell marked the spot for Fort Hall. The fort was named after Henry Hall, a backer of the expedition.

Ťhatháŋka Íyotake, better known as **Sitting Bull**

Chief Winnemucca also called Wobitsawahkah.

Hin-mah-too-yah-lat-kekt, popularly known as Chief Joseph

The Trail of Tears painting by Robert Lindneux

After Chief Sitting Bull led the Sioux against Custer's U.S. Cavalry at "The Battle of the Little Bighorn," the army bolstered the western troops with innumerable enlisted men, cannons, and new model repeating rifles. After many years of bloody battles the native people resigned themselves to the reservations, surrendered their weapons, horses and cattle.

The infamous "Trail of Tears" led the Cherokee to the U.S. government's Indian Territory west of the Mississippi and opened their land to settlement. To add insult to injury the settlers brought plagues of cholera, measles and smallpox, killing thousands. They wiped out the traditional game animals and systematically assassinated swaths of adult male family members.

John Ross
Also known as Guwisguwi, was the Principal Chief of the Cherokee Nation from 1828–1866.

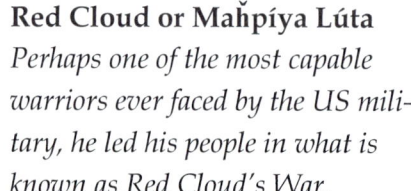**Red Cloud or Maȟpíya Lúta**
Perhaps one of the most capable warriors ever faced by the US military, he led his people in what is known as Red Cloud's War.

Tȟašúŋke Witkó
Better known as Crazy Horse, war chief of the Oglala Lakota led a war party to victory at the Battle of the Little Bighorn.

Goyaałé
Better known as Geronimo was a prominent war chief of the Apache during the Apache wars with Spain and Texas .

In the spring of 1879, after the Bannock Wars, the Little Camas Prairie was opened to settlement. Two brothers, James and Jared Peck, established a stage stop in Butte Springs, which later became the town of Crichton. Another stop that was established near the main soldier encampment became the town of Soldier, which the *Wood River Times* called "little New York."

"Main Street, Soldier" By Tami Peck

By 1897, Soldier, Idaho boasted 3,000 residents and was a hub for townships like Crichton, Corral, Cook, Taft, Fir Grove, Manard and Spring Creek, all of which supported their own stage stations, post offices and schools.

Not much of Crichton is left. The Peck family still owns a working farm on the old town site. Tami Peck was kind enough to give Maria and me a tour. The barn yard was full of relics, primitive tools and farm implements. The barn displayed horse and wagon tack, some of which was well over a hundred years old

Bannock warriors ambushed a wagon train at Massacre Rock near American Falls. The hostilities between pioneer and native people resulted in the need for a safer route.

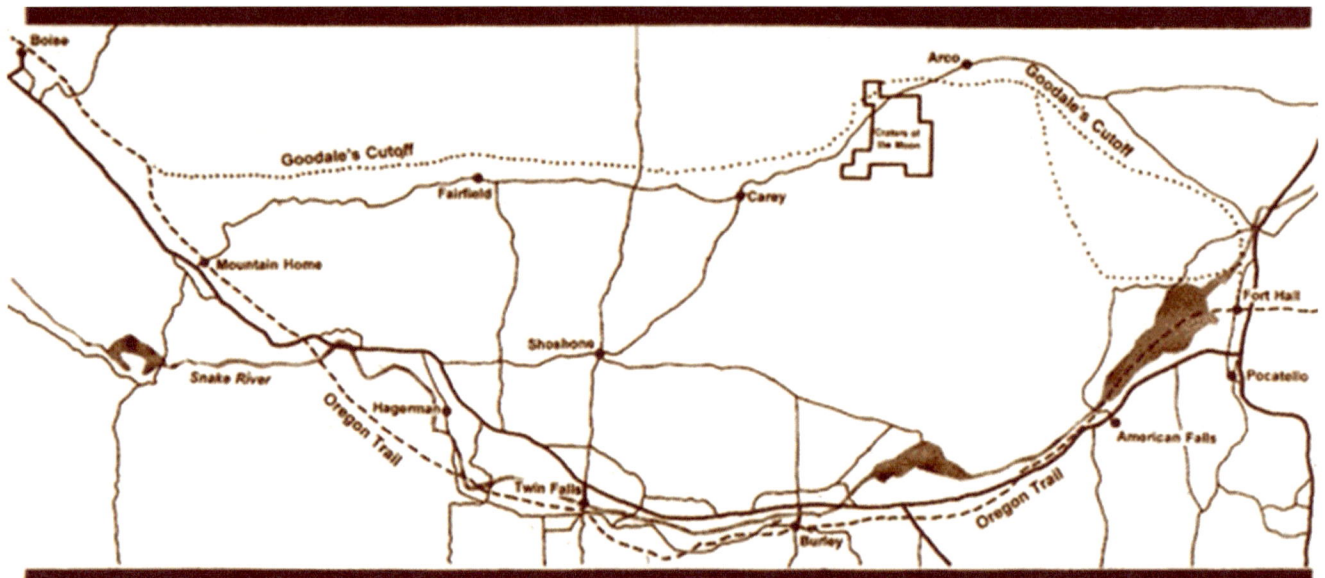

Tim Goodale was asked to guide the followers of the Oregon trail west from Fort Hall. They hoped the Bannock resistance on the alternate route would be reduced, and the cut off would give them easier access to the Salmon River gold fields.

You can still find remnants of Goodale's Cutoff

Goodale succeeded in leading the party of over one thousand people, more than three hundred wagons, and almost three thousand head of stock safely to Boise.

Surely the largest wagon train to ever venture on the Oregon Trail, the company was so big it took over three hours to get into or out of camp.

Many years ago, while drifting through Blackfoot, Idaho I joined an older Shoshone artisan setting on a bench in front of his curio shop/art studio. I was close to broke and hoping to find a little work. He enjoyed some whisky while I cleaned up his work area. After a few long pulls from his pocket flask he told me a story.

A Sho-Ban legend
as told by the Shoshone Artist.

Many years ago a brave hunter of the Bannock went to explore other lands and to find if there were other people on the earth. He went south for many days till he found a poor people who lived in a hot land. He married a beautiful woman of that people and stayed with her for many springs. He told the people of the hot land about his home, about the animals and waters, he told them about the tall grasses and trees but they did not believe him.

Because of the heat and the poor food he decided to take his family and started the long journey home. His wife's brothers wanted to go. "Show us this land and we will live there too." He agreed and was happy to take much of his new family to his people.

His wife's brothers had never seen a rabbit. They had eaten fish and frogs, they had eaten roots and seed but never had they hunted deer or elk and they had never hunted the buffalo.

On the trip the man became hungry. He saw a rabbit and took it for food. As he cooked the rabbit the brothers and his wife became afraid and hid from the cooking fire. He called to his wife to come and taste the meat; she liked it very much and did give meat to her brothers. They also liked the food. They asked their brother in-law to teach them to hunt for this good food.

The Bannock brave taught the brothers how to make the bow and how to make the arrows, he taught them how to hunt, how to dress the meat and how to make good of the skins.

As they traveled north they learned the skills of the Bannock and became good hunters, they learned to make the tools of hunting, and they learned to make moccasins for their feet and the tepee for their dwelling.

As the Bannock man and his family traveled, they met only enemies along the way. The Bannock brave taught his brother in-laws to fight. He taught the brothers how to hide from the enemy and how to leave no footprint.

The family traveled until they came to the Bannock people. They gathered around the chief's fire and held counsel in the chief's lodge where many braves told stories and smoked the pipe. The wife's brothers had never seen people smoking before. Their eyes stung and filled with tears. Finally, they stood up and left the lodge. Then the Bannock brave told his people about the young men. "They have hunted with me; we have made the bow together. They have fought my enemy and did not run. It is good that they stay with us."

The five brothers stayed in the north country for many springs. By the time they wanted to return to their people in the south, they could shoot with bows and arrows; they could kill rabbits and deer and buffalo; they knew how to cook the flesh of the animals. They had learned how to tan the skins and to make moccasins. How to make robes and dwellings from the buffalo hides. They taught their people in the south all those things. And now the people of the south live well.

By
David Eveningthunder

Treasures on the Camas Prairie

On our travels Maria and I often find treasures: Old store fronts, farmsteads, home sites and every once in a while, cool old relics of a bygone era.

A Soldier's View

Easy Going on the Camas Prairie
by ckevinswan

The doorknob came off in my hand but it did its job and the door of the shack pulled open with a loud squawk of distressed, unused hinges. My eyes quickly tightened to a squint in response to the bright, early spring sky as I stepped out to survey the frosted bunchgrass of the Camas Prairie.

I was lucky to find this wonderful old shambles of a homestead. The fireplace was usable and the wood of the fallen outbuildings made for a warm fire and a cozy place to throw camp for the night.

I was happy to see a line of trees and shrubs meander across the prairie floor just a couple hundred yards from the shack; fresh water from the Soldier Mountains would make for a good cup of coffee. I dug my always handy, dinted steel bucket from the truck and a handful of crackers from my duffle and headed toward the tree line.

Wasn't another house to be seen, not a power line, no hint of home or farm for as far as the eye could see. If it wasn't for the faint thunk, thunk, thunk of a distant tractor's motor wafting through the air, I would have thought I was all alone in the world.

Turned out the tree line was a little farther than I expected and I was well into a half-mile walk before I reached the crystalline, almost invisible water hurrying to its not-so-far-off destination of Wood River.

I usually don't drink water from an unknown source till I've boiled it and added coffee, but looking well up creek, all that could be seen were the trees that dressed this creek and the mountains that fathered it.

I dipped my bucket for a drink. Trout fry darted from my shadow, cold surged up the braided wire handle of my bucket, and the water rattled my teeth with cold as I drank; I liked it here.

After enjoying a big drink and a happily comfortable sit on a beaver-fell log, I started to notice movement. Shadow with flashes of red darted from creek bank to creek bank and the fancy of a trout breakfast replaced thoughts of Campbell's tomato soup.

I didn't even notice the walk back to the shack. After a hurried riffle of my duffle and a quick dodge to the back of my pickup seat, I was soon on my way back to the creek with size-8 fish hooks and a wrapped length of fish line I always carry for just such an occasion. Didn't take long to find a perfectly flexible willow switch and a few grubs dug from under the fallen log.

It wasn't hard to get comfortable. The sun cast nurturing warmth across my back, shadows of early season, un-leafed trees pushed in soothing patterns across the creek bank and the sound of the dancing water cooled my senses.

The trout were hungry and I soon had a nice huddle of pan-size fish gilled with a stick secured in the rocky bottom of the creek. "Four should be a good breakfast." I wasn't surprised to hear my own voice carry hollowly in the cool air but I was surprised by a low, horsy, grumble from the other side of the creek.

My eyes hurried to find a standing, angry black bear glaring at me. My muscles tightened with adrenalin as my eyes met his dark stare.

Again he grumbled. My hand slowly slipped to the grip of my belt knife and I readied myself for an assault. A greyed and scarred muzzle opened in an intimidating snarl, large paws baring long dark claws raked the air, my blood ran cold and thoughts of loved ones passed through my mind.

My voice lifted and shook, "You up for a fight, let's go!" The knife palmed securely, I stepped back, hoping to ease out of the situation. A tangle of branch and grass caught my foot, I lost my balance and in a desperate attempt to catch myself took an inadvertent step forward and was standing in the creek.

The bear must have thought I was on attack and almost fell to a sitting position; my fear was soon replaced with sympathy. This poor old fella didn't have the energy to fight, his chest was white with age and his attempt to intimidate only exposed a mouth full of aged teeth, black with decay at the gums.

I was pretty sure I could whip him and I think he was too. The heat of the situation eased, I felt my heart calm. "Hey buddy." I kept my voice even and hushed. "Bet you could use a little breakfast, huh?" My eyes fixed on the old timer and I slowly bent to gather my booty of gilled trout.

I knew why he was there; same reason I was. Fresh, clean water and the hope of easy food had brought both of us to this creek.

He wanted to bolt, he wasn't sure if he should run or attack but he didn't do either, he resigned himself to whatever fate was his. A big puff of vapored breath was followed by a snorty cough and I knew he was not only old but sick as well. "Dang man; you feeling bad fella? Let me help you out." I tossed the biggest of my catch to his side of the creek. He made a last attempt at intimidation, then slapped his large paw over the fish as a claim. After a few moments of investigating sniffs and oddly human yawning sounds he flopped to his belly and nuzzled the fish in joy of the free meal.

Grubs and worms from under the fallen logs were plentiful so I tossed my catch of the day to him and settled in to catch more. "Say ol fella; you look kinda beat up." I was still a little nervous with him but his attention was all about his breakfast. "You must be a few weeks out of hibernation. Bet some young bully pushed you off your range."

I stood carefully, still aware this was a bear no matter how old and torn up he was. I didn't turn my back on him as I stepped away from the creek bank and out of the tree line. He didn't pay more than a little attention but bid me farewell with his oddly human yawning sound.

The pen and ink drawings in this story are courtesy of Jerry Wilda

I was most of three quarters back to my squatted shack when I heard his yawning call behind me. I turned to address him, still some hundred yards back. He sat, lifted a paw. Almost like he was showing me he had no weapons. "I only got soup left, have it if you want, I guess." If he wasn't an old man it would have been a bad thing to let him associate food with people, it would only get him killed but I figured this was his last season of life and as I said before, I was almost sure I could whip him.

I turned and finished my walk to the shack, dropped the water and gathered wood from the fallen out-building; I figured I'd have some soup and crackers then find my way to Fairfield and a local grocery. He stood and watched as I drove off looking for town. I didn't think I would ever see him again and half-waved good bye.

I followed the loose dirt road to a highway. I enjoyed the valley as I drove, and stopped at a few farms along the way asking about work. Most folks were polite but unfriendly.

Must have been pretty obvious I was a drifter; people don't like drifters and most of the time they make it obvious. So, I wasn't confident of finding work but I still had a nice roll of money in my pocket from work in the Bear Lake area of Idaho.

I'm not sure how serious I was about finding work, but thought I'd look; who knows, might find some good duty or make a friend.

Fairfield didn't have much to offer as far as groceries go but it did have staples: bag of potatoes, various vegetables, some onions and garlic and fresh hamburger. I figured a nice stew would bless my bones.

Asked about work as I checked out at the counter but the teller didn't say much, pointed vaguely west, mumbled something about farmers and early spring. I did get a bushel of leftover, wintered apples and several bags of older baked goods from the discount basket thinking I could leave them near the creek for my ailing buddy bear.

Still brisk with early spring, wind pushed through the open window of my pickup, making the thermos of hot coffee a real treat, and I enjoyed every sip as I crisscrossed the wide river bottom valley looking for work.

Snow gleamed from the north slope of the rolling hills that soon evolved into the Sawtooth Mountain Range, fifty or so miles away. A wonderful tapestry of land, woven of snow-covered mountains, rich deep soil and slowly rolling creeks made for a wonderful cruise.

Sparsely populated farm and ranch land, high sage desert and alpine mountain sat within just a few miles of each other and the whole of the area would surprise with cold, deep, still pools of cloudy gray water and a stretch of marshland rich with life. On that very drive, pronghorn antelope bounded from the approach of my truck, eagles and hawks searched for their lunch from an Idaho blue sky, whitetail and mule deer stomped their cloven feet as I passed, a large herd of elk and cattle all but ignored my cloud of road dust when I pulled into a feed lot still full with wintered cattle.

I was lucky to find the farmer, who lay awkwardly over the front tire of a tractor, head half - buried in the engine compartment, hands full with tractor parts and wrenches.

I walked to a position beside the tractor that would give him a clear view of me while he worked. "I'm looking for work." He lifted his eyes from the belly of the red Farmall tractor and smiled.

"I got work fer a fella knows how to throw feed and pull calves." His eyes returned to follow a wrench to its task of fighting a stubborn bolt. "Pays better if he can drive a tractor."

He started to reach to his tool box with an uncomfortable stretch; I hefted the tool box closer for him. "Yea, I can drive a tractor, I've worked plenty of feedlots and dairies, feed mill, med shoots; I know the work." Seeing his next reach to the tool box would be for a ratchet and deep socket, I handed him the set. "I'm just passing through, not looking for a job, just work."

"Camas Night"

Crisp blue eyes nesting in heavy lids, wrinkled with many years of sun, smiled. He stretch and rocked his back as he stood from the front tire of his tractor. "Don't get many bums around these parts. Fair warnin' son, folks about here don't like thieves."

At first, I wanted to be offended, but it was obvious this was a hardworking man who didn't have time in his life for guile; I took his warning to heart. "Well, I'm no thief, I won't bother anyone."

"Tel-ya wat; my son is leaving for the mission field this Sunday, I got a couple hands comin', won't be maybe, two weeks." His eyes drifted over the valley floor to rest on Smokey Dome as he talked. "Work till then, come to church Sundays and I'll give ya twenty-two dollar a day. You can fill yer truck from the tanks near the truck yard Sunday after late feed and b'for you leave." He wiped his broad calloused hand on a striped coverall and extended it to me. We shook hands.

"OK; I'll be here Sunday. What time do you get home from church?"

He turned his attention back to his engine work. "You know the deal son; be at the white community church, Main Street, Fairfield, Sunday, nine mornin'. Don' worry bout being dressed up, just Camas folks, potluck after church, then we'll come do a feed together and I'll show you chores yu'al be doin'."

I felt myself smile. "Yes sir." He looked up just long enough to meet my smile with one of his own. "Sunday, white church, downtown Fairfield; I'll be there." Just a short conversation but I liked this guy and as I drove from his farm I felt good about our deal.

After doing a slow cruise of both city blocks in Fairfield, I easily found the church. A nice little place, colonial looking, neat and well kept.

A Waylon Jennings song clouded with stale cigarette smoke drifted from the open doors of a saloon just across the street and half a block closer to the Camas County Courthouse. A well-groomed, preacher-looking fella waved to a man sweeping the sidewalk just outside the bar and bounded up the steps of the church and through the doors.

I might have done better to stop and visit the pastor of the church but found myself parked in front of the bar.

I wondered if I made a mistake when I stepped into the darkness of that bar. Sunlight   followed me through the door, filtered through the honky-tonk haze and lay in rectangular patterns across the floor. Every head turned from the mirrored back wall to watch the big, long-haired stranger belly up to the bar and ask for a draft beer.

"I'll buy the hippy a beer." The drink-slurred voice cast over the last few notes of the Waylon Jennings song. The song ended and the voice fell at almost the same time, leaving an odd silence in the air.

The bartender pushed the beer in front of me. I lifted it to salute the buyer of a free beer and enjoyed a nice big gulp.

"You need a haircut."

I started counting heads in the mirror and wondered how many assailants I would have.

An old man farmer and an equally aged date were closest to me. His head fell and his attention focused on the beer bottle in his hand. Three other farmer-capped heads and two cowboy hats. "Wonder if that big boy squats ta pee?" I knew the trouble was coming from the cowboys. My eyes searched the mirror behind the bar looking for the emanation of the voice. "You squat ta pee fella?" I knew right then this wasn't going to go well. "You some kinda funny boy?" There was no reason to pretend he was just poking fun; the man was drunk and looking for trouble.

I picked up my beer and stepped between obvious farmers and the cowboys, with my attention on the one verbalizing his disapproval of my long, pony-tailed hair.

I didn't say anything but focused my attention on his eyes. My direct confrontation caught the slim, smallish cowboy by surprise; his eyes pulsed with anticipation as his hands rose in surrender. "Hold on there fella, I was just poking fun, ain't no reason to get wound up."

I was careful to keep my voice steady and low. "No problem. Just came to drink my beer and buy you one in return." My eyes turned to the fully attentive crowd in the mirror.

The bartender stepped to our end of the bar. "You best have your drink and move on buddy." It was obvious I wasn't welcome and actually I was a little glad of it; bars have always been nothing but trouble for me.

Downing my beer and leaving without another word seemed like my best option and I did.

A great junk store presented itself just as I was turning from Main Street to the highway to head to the shack I called home. A rather used recliner sat prominently in the window with a sign "$7.00." I soon had the chair, and a tattered, oval, braided rug, and several other castaway items in the back of my truck along with a shiny, almost new coffee pot.

The beauty of the Camas Prairie and the blue of the sky soon washed the bar from my mind; I enjoyed the drive to my shack, then toted the stale baked goods and crate of apples to the creek to leave for the old bear.

After returning to the shack and setting a fire, the smell of a hamburger stew mixed with the wonderful aroma of percolating coffee. I was almost delighted to sit in the newly acquired recliner with my sketch pad and a cup of real perked coffee. Working on a sketch of a fella I buddied with for a while on the east side of the country must have soothed me enough to drift into a nap.I was woken by the sound of the old bear snorting around the shack's door; I knew it was him by the now familiar, odd yawning sound.

The stew was done, maybe a little overdone but it smelled great and was probably why the ol fella was snorting around the door.

Scooping a heaping portion of the stew into a recently emptied coffee can seemed like the neighborly thing to do; I was reasonably sure he had already eaten the goods left for him at the creek, but a hot hamburger stew is hard to pass up and almost impossible not to share.

By
ckevinswan
www.ckevinswan.com

When I pulled the door open he backed off a few yards then lazily flopped to his butt. His nose twitched and head lifted, looking for the source of the wonderful smell.

I set the can of stew as close as I dared, then returned to push the coffee back on to a newly stocked fire and filled a bowl of the stew for myself. For the next few minutes my companion and I snorted and slopped stew.

I didn't pay much attention as I ate; the old bear finished his dinner and wandered off in the direction of the creek.

I finished the picture of Speedy Mike and closed the door. The fire was soothing; a full belly, and the comfortable chair made for a restful night.

I woke once, very early in the morning and stepped outside for a pee. My buddy bear was just outside the door. He followed me to the outbuildings and watched me gather wood then wandered off in the direction of the creek again. "See you later." He turned and snorted. His oddly human yawn seemed like a reply as he disappeared across the prairie into the early morning dark. I returned to the recliner, stocked the fire and finished a good night's sleep.

I knew working for the farmer wouldn't allow much sightseeing so I spent the next few days poking around the backlands and dirt roads. When I shopped, I always kept my friend bear in mind and bought day-old baked goods and fruit.

He seemed to show up just in time for dinner every night , and although I always kept my distance it was nice to have company.

It became a ritual that he would join me at the outbuildings every morning. We would both do our business, then he would wander in the general direction of the creek and I would start getting ready for my day.

My last day of freedom before reporting to Sunday church as I agreed wasn't any different. I came home from town with some fresh groceries, my buddy lay comfortably several yards from the shack enjoying a nap in the sun. I worked on a picture in front of the fire, and all was well on the Camas Prairie.

I got up to go for the morning ritual and even talked to the ol fella as I walked outside but he wasn't there. I walked the field to the creek and found him curled in a thicket of aspen trees. "Hey! What's up buddy, need a few extra winks this morning?" I stepped as close as I dared. "Bear?" I was careful to keep my voice easy, I trusted the ol fella but he was still a wild bear. "Bear?" He was gone; passed in the night. I felt a sinking in my heart and was surprised to feel tears grow in my eyes. Spent the most of that morning digging a grave for the ol fella; made sure he was comfortable on the braided rug, then cobbled a little cross for his grave.

End

Willow Creek

Cabin on Camas Series #2 of 5

When I find a cool old place like the one pictured in my Cabin on Camas Series, I make many trips to the location for several years and through all four seasons, to create a representational collection of images that captures its personality.

Camas County is a bit more than 120 miles from my home. Maria and I traveled there 30 times over a three-year period and have collected well over 100 photos of this one cabin.

"Uncle Bill's"

Break from the hunt by ckevinswan

I encourage everyone to spend a few days on the back-roads of Camas County. Remember, folks on the Camas tend to be a little stranger-shy and protective of property and privacy. Bring a lunch, few services are available so be prepared and bring your camera…. because it is nice.

From the high grasslands of the Camas Prairie, wagon trains following Goodale's Cutoff dropped into the Snake River Plain west of Mountain Home near Canyon Creek and entered a sheltered area called Round Canyon. It offered year-round running water, protection from heavy weather and, depending on the time of year, vendors of goods and services.

Canyon Creek Station then and now

Sometime in 1872, Archie and Harriet Daniel homesteaded Canyon Creek and built a two-structure stage stop with rocks quarried from the canyon's walls.

I've seen the same two-building layout many times. One building, usually the smaller, was used as a kitchen/utility room and the other for stage passenger comforts and upstairs housing for the proprietor. Often a covered breezeway was constructed between the buildings, to allow stage passengers to step from stage to station while protected from the weather.

Canyon Creek Station was in full operation until 1921. The Southern Idaho stage stops closed down as paved roads and railways expanded through the west.

This wonderful old barn is found just feet from the trail, a few miles west of Mayfield

From Canyon Creek, pioneers joined the main route of the Oregon Trail, which led into the Boise Valley. The flatland crossing into and through the valley was a welcome respite from the still-wild and often-hostile country of south-central Idaho.

In 1833, Captain Bonneville first looked over the Boise Valley a few miles west of the future site of Mayfield and dubbed it, "Les Bois." One of the earliest written references to Euro-American dwellings east of Fort Boise mentions Mayfield but only a few ruins now stand as evidence that anyone was ever there.

In 1844, the Hudson Bay Company followed in Bonneville's path, and the Fort Boise trading post was constructed. Ten years later, the earliest wagon trains found their way to the valley along the same route, which had been dubbed the Oregon Trail.

The area east of Boise through Parma, Idaho is chock-full of historical sights and museums. It would take a large library to hold all the books that have been published about the early pioneers and settlers of Idaho's Treasure Valley, so I'm going to bypass that well-traveled road and start my story where the pioneers entered the Valley of Plenty.

Sweet Idaho Project
by ckevinswan

"Star Too." The mountain in the background is Squaw Butte (Woman's Mountain)

Emmett, Idaho has long been one of my favorite places to start a day trip. Poking around the grasslands of Squaw Butte (Woman's Mountain) and Gem County's yonderlands for the project in this issue was a lot of fun. Beautiful landscapes, intriguing histories, and a rich collection of original settlers' homes and old buildings inspired many representational works of art and short stories in this volume.

Maria and I were cruising alongside the Payette River on one of those day trips. It was a beautiful early spring day, perfect for seeking adventure. We were hoping to find a road we had never been on before as we followed the Payette River and Highway 52 east towards Horseshoe Bend. The trip was enjoyable but there wasn't anything to get excited about until we came to one of Idaho's best-kept secrets, The Sweet/Ola Highway.

I have turned north on that highway a couple of times, once when I was working as casual labor hand for a freight delivery company and once during a teen party with some buddies, but I never had a chance to look around.

At first impression, the narrow valley that follows Squaw (Woman's) Creek is much like other creek runs of the Payette—nice. There is some BLM land scattered through the hills but its mostly privately owned farmlands or ranches. The people of Gem County and land following the creek runs that make up Woman's Creek water shed are carful of their property and privacy but welcoming and friendly.

"End of Woman's Creek"

I knew there were a couple of small communities on the comfortable country road but as we followed the eastern slope of Squaw Butte north into backlands and high prairie, we found a part of the world where GOD takes his morning walk: Idaho at her finest.

Squaw Creek starts way off and gone, in the backlands of Gem County's panhandle, and ends its run at the Payette River near the beginning of Black Canyon Reservoir. The small valley that follows the creek run offers intriguing history of frontiersman, pioneers and, of course, Native Americans. The first written records date back into the early 1800s but it was peaceful country until gold was discovered at the Thunder Mountain Mine.

Folklore tells us the butte was named by Weiser Shoshone families who used the area as their winter resort. "Squaw Butte," a poor translation for what should be "Woman's Mountain" in English, reaches almost six thousand feet at its highest point, runs roughly north to south and is a little over eight miles long.

Near Timber Butte

"Color on Timber Butte"

The top of the Sweet/Ola Highway

Farmstead
at
Sweet, Idaho

Farmsteads of Woman's Creek

*Farmstead
at
Timber Butte*

The area was a perfect summering land. When hunting parties went into the uplands, the men would leave their wives and children along the creek for the clean water, plentiful food gathering, and easy fishing.

While I was visiting the Gem County Museum I was lucky enough to meet a grand old fellow who loved to tell stories. And of course, I love to listen.

When the leading south ridge of the butte is seen from a distance, it's easy to imagine the face of a woman crying.

The Woman's Mountain Morns

As told by a Gem County history buff

There was no war with us; all of the True People of this Land were at peace. We were happy.

A family came to hunt. The wives and children stayed near the waters at the mountain of women. They stayed to gather food and to fish while men went to the mountain to hunt. Because the men knew there was no war, they slept in comfort under the stars and did not fear for their families. They hunted the grasslands for many days.

The wives made baskets for the children so they could sleep in the shade of trees while the wives and daughters fished and gathered foods from the valley.

The daughters heard men's voices that spoke with unknown words; they hurried to tell the women. Then the daughters and women returned in quiet to the children.

They heard the strangers near where their babies and small children slept. They gathered their children to them and went to the Woman's Mountain to hide.

The men with strange words were hunting on the Woman's Mountain. They saw the wives and the daughters and the children and followed. They slew the wives, the daughters, and children with knives and clubs. The men with strange words murdered the families with cruelty and no regret.

The Woman's Mountain cried to the Great Spirit for the lost people. The heaven heard the cry and the earth's wrath followed the strangers.

The strangers lost their lives without pride and ended in brutal deaths.

The Woman's Mountain had her justice, but still she morns the loss of her children. Look to her face against the blue sky. She cries even now to the heavens.

David Eveningthunder's art is in tribute to the contemporary dancers who keep the traditions of his people alive

The hunters in the legend may have been Weiser River Shoshone. It is said the 1854 Ward Massacre was an attack of revenge by the Shoshone as the result of their families being slaughtered on Woman's Mountain. The Shoshone warriors were, of course, infuriated and let loose their anger, killing all but a few of the Ward Party. Fifteen-year-old William Ward took an arrow through the lung. Surprisingly, he survived by hiding in the brush until the war party left, and then found his way to Fort Boise.

The U.S. Army eventually caught up with the Shoshone war party and executed eighteen warriors—the same number killed in the Ward wagon train. The Ward Massacre occurred about twelve miles south of Woman's Mountain, near the Boise River. Maria and I often stop at the massacre's memorial park near Middleton, Idaho before we venture into the Woman's Mountain area.

By David Eveningthunder

David Eveningthunder

Many Shoshone families lived along the Payette River and throughout the area now called Gem County. They spoke a dialect of Uto-Aztecan and lived in grass huts called wickiups. Led by Chief Eagle Eye, they were friendly people who sought peace and traded goods with neighboring tribes, establishing councils and powwows at several locations along the Weiser and Snake Rivers. The most notable were held at Council, Idaho and in nearby Indian Valley.

Buffalo hides, horses, and salmon were favored trading goods among all the people, who also traded hunting and war implements: arrowheads, arrows, bows, and knives. Some tribes brought cedar lodge poles and others brought raw obsidian to be flaked for making utensils that could cut and scrape.

All were welcomed: Nez Perce, Northern Paiute, Arapahoe, Cheyenne, Umatilla, Cayuse, and many others took advantage of the councils to trade their wares.

Euro-American settlers referred to the people who followed Eagle Eye as "Weiser Shoshone"or "Sheepeaters." They called themselves "Tukudika," which I'm told means "Eaters of Mountain Sheep."

The story of Eagle Eye and his people is intriguing because they were able to live freely when most other Native American people had already resigned themselves to reservation life. They were also the only native people able to avoid conflict with the United States military during the Snake War, headed by General George Crook, and to avoid capture during the Sheepeater Campaign of 1879.

I'm told the last of the free Shoshone lived in the area of Dry Buck and Timber Butte close to Woman's Mountain near Sweet. When it became necessary, Eagle Eye and his people joined the settlers of Emmett and worked in the mining and timber industries.

I've read as many histories of Chief Eagle Eye as I could find. He was a brilliant man, a man of peace and patience. Stories are told that he carved wooden images for tribal children as he sat at the door of his wickiup. When he carved, his people gathered by his fire and listened to his life's teachings. Truly a man of honor, he passed away at the end of May 1896. In 1904, the last of his Weiser band transitioned to the Fort Hall Indian Reservation.

Chief Eagle Eye was the last leader of the Shoshone people before they were constrained to reservation life

Paintings by Jay Anderson

Woman's Creek falls off the Western Range of the Central Mountains.

"Jerusalem Valley"
by ckevinswan

Jerusalem Valley is found just a few miles East of Squaw Butte, and North of Horseshoe Bend, on Highway 55. The beautiful and hidden little valley follows a collection of creek runs as they fall out of the Boise Central Mountains

Lost in Jerusalem

By ckevinswan

A little time working for a road maintenance crew in eastern Idaho made for a nice, fat wallet and it was time to visit my mom and my home town. Wasn't any reason to hurry, jobs were plentiful for a big, young guy with a strong back and Mom would always open her door for me.

When I did finally reach Nampa my brother already had a job lined up. I got home on a Thursday night, spent a couple of days at Mom's and started working for a bricklayer Monday morning just a couple of miles north of Horseshoe Bend.

We'd been on the job site for most of two weeks the first time I walked up Porter Creek Road and was struck by the beauty of the green, rolling hills and the bounty of that little area of the Payette River Valley called Jerusalem.

My brother warned me the guy couldn't keep help and it didn't take me long to understand why. He was always yelling and often called me names.

One especially nice day the bricklayer was taking a hangover out on me. I didn't like the guy and was looking for a reason to find something else to do. After a brutal tirade about his mortar being too wet, I had enough, took my lunchbox and walked off, didn't know where I was, kinda had an idea but had never been in that part of the world before, so I chose the first road that looked like it would go somewhere and left the frustrated bricklayer to his own devices.

It was a wonderful day; the birds were singing, flowers blooming and the hills were as green as any I have ever seen. I was having such a great day that I lost track of time. It was late afternoon before I noticed the hills around me still had snow tucked into the shadows. I turned to survey the land and found myself completely out of touch with any semblance of mankind. "No big thing." I sat to eat my now soggy sandwich and finish a thermos of coffee. "I'll just head back down the road. I couldn't have walked too far." After the short rest I dusted myself off and headed down the little rutted road, back to Jerusalem Valley; I thought.

The sun began getting away from me as I came to a fork in the road. I didn't notice the split before but decided I would just keep to the road that seemed to be going downhill. After a mile or so I wasn't going down anymore and in fact found myself walking just a few hundred yards from the snowline.

This time of year that meant I was high, maybe five thousand feet or more. It was cool enough now that the jacket I'd been carrying was a pleasure to slip on.

"Together" by ckevinswan

I wondered if I should turn back to find the fork in the road again but thought it would be simpler to go straight downhill. My vision of the horizon was blocked but I was sure it was just that one hill and I would soon be able to see the river and maybe even Horseshoe Bend on just the other side. That one hill turned into another, then another, and now it was getting dark. I was tired and I have to tell you: I was more than a little uncomfortable with my circumstances. I've been lost more than a couple of times in my life. Being a single guy with no responsibilities and about half-hobo, I haven't ever really cared where I spent the night but something about being alone on a cold, dark, landscape with no idea which direction to turn, made the night even colder. It was one of the few times in my life I really felt lost.

It was dark. I figured it was after eleven and of course, when things go wrong, they all go wrong. There was no sky. I had watched over the past few hours as a heavy cloud cover came across the high grassland and hillsides of scrub brush.

Little to use for fire, nothing to use for shelter, and the coyotes crying from the surrounding hills gave me the feeling of an old Dracula movie. All I could do was sit on the ground and wait for morning. I pulled my arms inside my jacket and braced for a long night; it was.

A couple of times in the night I thought I saw the ghost of lights cross the hillside a mile or so away. I decided that was the direction I would go at first light.

The morning was coming slowly, I was wet from dew but it hadn't rained. It felt good to get off of the cold ground and stretch but that's the only positive thing I have to say about the beginning of the new day. Well, that and nothing ate me in the night.

Easy country to get lost in high grassland of a rolling prairie landscape, I should know I've been lost twice on the Camas and once on the Palouse

Setting in the grasses of the Camas, Prairie, on a spring day with a light breeze is a balm that sooths the soul and quickens the mind. Like staring at the stars it lets you know how vast this world is.

I headed in the direction of the passing lights. Maybe I would see a distant road. It was   so cloudy, if it hadn't been early morning I wouldn't have known the sun was on my left. I was walking south and found some encouragement in that. Uncertain of how it had happened I was walking just a few hundred feet from the forest. I know southern Idaho enough that heading south along the tree line was a good sign, it probably meant I was within a few miles of people, although it did seem like civilization was hiding from me.

"HEY! YOU!" I was so happy to hear a voice; it didn't bother me that the voice sounded angry.

"Hey! You just stand right the hell there." I turned to see an old fella about half bent with age. "What are you doing on my   property?" The old guy was hard to see under a dirty green baseball cap and black, thick-framed glasses hanging on the end of a whisky drinker's red nose. I didn't see a gun and I felt wonderful about this old man yelling at me. "How the hell did you get on the back of my property?!"

"I don't know." I tried to sound friendly, because he wasn't happy about me being on his land. "I walked up from Jerusalem Valley."

The old fella's face changed. His poorly fit dentures looked from a distance like a smile. "You did not!?" As he talked, his dirty brown, debris-filled dentures stuck a half inch past his bottom lip and the thick horned rim glasses bobbed up and down with each word.

I opened my hands as I walked toward him and was careful not to hurry. His green and black flannel shirt was just as old and crusty as he was. It was patched in several spots and darned with various colored threads. "I spent the night on the hills back there and could sure use some water."

I stopped about ten feet short of him. I could smell the old fella better than I could see him. His worn and tattered blue jeans were heavy with dirt; it took a belt and crossed suspenders to hold them up.

A big unbelieving grin grew and filled his face. "So you tellin' me you walked across Jackass Basin yesterdee?" He pushed his glasses up on the bridge of his nose and I realized his smile was more like a grimace. "Betcha yur thirsty." He turned and motioned me to follow as he stuck a thumb under one suspender. "Hungry too ain't cha? Come along then, I got coffee on." The old fella struggled up the steep hill. "You're lucky I like ta pee outdoors kiddo, still a mile or so to Harris Creek Road."

I wasn't sure about eating anything this old fella offered but the coffee sounded good so up the hill I followed. Wasn't more than fifty yards to the top of the hill and we were looking at the back of an old shack just as crusty and bent as the fella I was following.

"Harris Creek Road?" I knew the bricklayer stopped at Harris Creek Road to adjust the toolbox after hitting some hard frost heaves coming down Horseshoe Bend Pass and I now had a good idea where I was. "Jackass Basin, Is that the hollow just a mile or so back?" I could smell fresh coffee as we started across a mostly empty woodshed/back porch. I liked the crusty new friend better every foot closer to that coffee. "I think I spent the night there."

The old feller had to jerk the back door open to pull the bottom corner through a ridge of mud, woodchips and pine bark. The door was patched at least twice with plywood and it looked like a wire held it together from the inside top corner to the outside bottom. The floor of the old shack might have been wood but had been layered with dirt for some time. An oval braided rug covering the used -to-be wood floor was so caked with dirt that I couldn't tell what color it was.

As the door shut it left most of the light behind. It took a few minutes for my eyes to adjust to the darkness and my nose to adjust to the textures of odors that filled the main room of the small house. When the old fella pulled a cup from open-shelved cupboards I'm almost sure I saw something move. "I got sugar if you want." He pointed at the pump on the side of a rusted, cast metal sink. "Water up here is the best. You'll want some but first have some coffee and a biscuit." He must have known what I was going to say. "My sister makes me some bread and biscuits every week." He poured steaming hot coffee from a stovetop coffee percolator. The handle had been repaired with a tree limb and wire; the top fell off as he poured. "Damn that's hot!" he replaced the top. He looked at me over the top of his glasses and gave me the half smile, half grimace as he handed me the cup and a biscuit. "You'll like them biscuits."

He was right. That just may have been the best biscuit I'd ever had. Coffee, biscuit and a big daub of honey and I was ready for whatever was next on the old man's agenda. It wasn't long before I found out what that was.

"Come on, I wanna show you somethin'." We walked back out the same way we came in, but this time we went across the leveled area of his home-site and up the hill again.

At the top of the hill, we stopped at an area he had flattened with a shovel and added what flat rocks he could find. From our vantage point, we looked out over the not-so-distant features and creeks that made up Jerusalem Valley and the Boise Central Mountains. It was beyond beautiful.

Directly ahead of us was Mariah Mountain. My new friend pointed at each peak, every wash and creek run. "That's Porter Creek." He rolled the names like a poem, his bent finger dancing like a maestro's wand as he pointed. "Brynor Creek, Howley Mountain, Jackass Basin." Every place he pointed out was beautiful and had a story.

As we visited and he pointed, I learned he was one of the last keepers of the old Harris Creek Tollgate and he had lived his life on that mountain.

"Well, heck; I guess you'll be wantin' a ride? I can only take you as far as the Horseshoe Bend highway, but you'll find people there."

We took a little path around the hill and back down to the front of his property. An old Ford pickup, as crusty and unkempt as the shack and the old man waited in an almost driveway. The old man whistled and we were joined by an ugly, one-eyed blue heeler named Dog, and a wonderful black lab named Jake. Each dog nuzzled my friend and then jumped in the back of the truck. Jake, white-muzzled and obviously a longtime companion, had to have a little help.

The old beater started with little complaint and we headed down Harris Creek Road. After a short stop at the former tollgate site, we continued the pleasant ride to Horseshoe Bend Highway.

I've always been a little sorry I didn't get his name; never saw him again, in fact last I saw of him, Dog had his head out the passenger side window of the truck, tongue and tail wagging and Jake sat like a girlfriend beside the smelly, little old man.

I started the long walk up Horseshoe Bend pass heading home, thumb out. A red wing black bird sang to me as I walked past.

End

"Off the Tracks (Kim's Choice)"

"A Sweet Place"

Images along the Sweet/ Ola Byway. "Sweet Breeze"

"Rest" by ckevinswan

Looking east across the Camas Prairie

"Dressed in Green" by ckevinswan

Boise Basin

Gem of the Payette, Garden at the Butte, Valley of Plenty, and Gem County. Over the years, people who have called the area home have described it as an oasis. But it was not undiscovered country.

People from all across the land and as far away as China traveled by steamer up the Columbia River to Umatilla, departing from Umatilla by stage lines, and finally journeying by pack-train to the Boise Basin.

Inspired by a Native American legend of gold that could be scooped up by the handful, a party of prospectors led by George Grimes made the first gold strike in the Boise Basin in 1862 and were soon followed by a stampede of opportunists and wealth hunters.

Towards the end of 1863, an estimated twenty thousand people were scattered through the hills near Idaho City, including the communities of Centerville, Pioneerville, and Placerville, with thousands more in the prospective fields north of Emmett.

During the gold rush, Thunder Mountain, Liberty Mines, and hundreds of small operations depended on Sweet (named by its first postmaster, Ezekiel Sweet) as a supply stop for freight wagons. The town offered the services of hotels, saloons, a bank, a newspaper and, of course, a brothel. Roadhouses sprang up along every route and trail leading in and out of that gem of a valley.

One of my favorite historical stories takes place in that garden area along the Payette River, at the infamous roadhouse of the Picket Corral Gang.

4 to 1 odds by Jay Anderson

Downtown
Placerville, Idaho

The Picket Corral Gang
As told by L.A Gordon

The story begins with one word: *GOLD!* That word conjured images of riches beyond imagination, as well as new beginnings for those who panned the rivers of Idaho for the elusive yellow nuggets. Such imagery brought thousands of immigrants west in search of their fortunes.

Among them was David C. Updyke, born in 1830 to a prominent family near Cayuga Lake, New York. Early in life, Dave fell in with the wrong crowd. His parents soon grew tired of his shenanigans and asked him to leave, so he headed west, to California. He arrived about ten years too late for the gold rush of 1849, but his time in San Francisco wasn't wasted. He learned the art of creating bogus gold dust by galvanizing lead shavings with just enough gold to trick an assayer's test.

With the California gold fields all but depleted, he headed for new horizons: the burgeoning gold rush of Idaho's Boise Basin. In Idaho, he worked the Ophir Mine, and put together a nice stake of almost sixteen hundred dollars. He put that money to good use, buying a livery stable and saloon in the booming western town of Boise City. His saloon quickly attracted rough characters, some of whom joined what was to become the infamous Updyke Gang.

Updyke was a bright man who easily recognized his ilk. He made allies of the Stewart brothers, Alex and Charlie, who operated the Washoe Ferry on the Snake River between Idaho and Oregon. These brothers began transporting rustled cattle and stock animals into Oregon for Updyke's gang. They would steal stock animals from the Oregon locals and then transport the ill-gotten herds to Idaho, often stashing them at the now-legendary Picket Corral near Emmett.

*Single Log Fort
by Jay Anderson*

"Savin Scalp" by Jay Anderson

Picket Corral was a natural lava formation on the valley's steep eastern slope fenced with driftwood pickets that had been gleaned from the banks of the Payette River and lashed together, forming a barrier almost ten feet tall. The pickets spanned the hollow of the lava formation, creating a screened hiding place for the stolen animals. The herds were then taken by night over the hills into Horseshoe Bend and finally to the Boise Valley for resale.

Others of Updyke's cronies built a roadhouse that offered boarding to travelers on the stage route between Emmett and Horseshoe Bend. The unsuspecting guests would deposit their bags of gold dust with the inn for safekeeping but by night, the gang would replace upwards of half the travelers' gold with bogus gold dust. The scheme was so good, it could fool almost anyone.

Another enterprising sort, who had a dramatic run-in with the Updyke Gang, was William John McConnell. At twenty-three, McConnell had spent part of the late-1850s in California and later was in Oregon. He had discovered that selling vegetables to the hapless miners often netted more money than panning for those elusive nuggets. Upon hearing of Idaho's gold rush, he and his partner, John Porter, left Oregon and headed for Horseshoe Bend with a pan of onion sets, or seeds, given to them by their landlord. Homesteading the area that is now Jerusalem Valley, they planted the onion sets. After harvesting their bounty, they took it to Idaho City (then called Bannock), where miners paid top dollar for vegetables.

Both McConnell and Porter did well with their produce venture, but then came a problem: horse thieves were helping themselves to the stock animals of miners, ranchers and, of course, onion farmers.

McConnell took his dilemma to David Updyke, who was at that time the duly elected sheriff of Ada County. Of course, Updyke protected his band of outlaws, saying that he would see to the matter presently. Which, of course, he never did.

In the Hackamore by Jay Anderson

While going about his business in Boise City, McConnell happened on one of his stolen mares while boarding his horse in Updyke's livery stable. McConnell took Updyke to court over the stolen mare but fell prey to a kangaroo court full of Updyke's ruffians, ending up paying not only full value for the mare but back livery costs as well.

Upon arriving back at Horseshoe Bend with the recovered horse, McConnell and a man named Paddock held a meeting attended by local farmers, ranchers and townsfolk who had all grown weary of the general lack of law enforcement. They formed what was called the Payette Vigilance Committee of which McConnell was elected as their Captain.

There were three forms of punishment chosen by the group. Banishment from the country never to return was the least harsh, followed by public horsewhipping, then hanging as the most severe.

The group decided no matter what it cost or how long it took, they would rid themselves of bogus gold dust dealers, the Stewart brothers and of course Sheriff Updyke.

Many of the bogus gold dust deals were caught, found guilty and banished.

The Stewart brothers posted flyers in Horseshoe Bend and Boise City taunting the Committee saying there weren't enough of them to capture the ferry.

William McConnell and several others decide the flyer should be answered and on a snowy afternoon pointed their horses toward the ferry with a plan to take the Stewart brothers. One of the riders was unknown to the Stewarts so he was appointed to start the plan in action by going to their home.

He knocked loudly. Charley Stewart cracked the door slightly to investigate the knock and asked the man what he wanted.

The man pretended to be with his family and desperately needed to get to Boise as soon as possible offering to pay double the going rate. Charley happily opened the door.

Pretending to be cold, the man walked to the shelter's fireplace and casually added kindling to the flames, then stirring the embers created a flurry of sparks, signaling his waiting compatriots. The posse immediately charged through the door with shotguns drawn. Thus the ferry was taken without a punch thrown or a shot fired. Two of the three problems were now taken care of.

The young Stewart brothers from Canada were the original owners and operators of the Washoe Ferry Because of exposure to attack from the warring Paiute and Shoshone the isolated ferry-house was built like a fort and equipped to resist assault or withstand a siege for many days

Rope Ferry illustration, National Archives

Updyke, now not only the elected sheriff but also the Ada County tax collector, was taken into custody by the county commissioners for embezzling. He was tried, found guilty, and ordered to re-pay the stolen funds. He resigned as sheriff and, in fear for his life, he and the other remaining ruffian, Jake Dixon, left town, unaware they were being followed by the Payette Vigilance Committee. The posse caught up with the villains at Syrup Creek on the toll road to Rocky Bar, near Goodale's Cutoff of the Oregon Trail.

Horse theft and embezzling were just two of the crimes he was hung for that night. He died without a word. Dixon escaped, but was soon caught and hung also. Thus ended the reign of Sheriff Updyke and the Picket's Corral Gang.

There is a lot more to the story of Sheriff David Updyke than can be told in one setting. These stories are better told in the upcoming addition to this series, The Four Rivers Project

Harris Creek Station was an important stop on the stage route from Horseshoe Bend to Idaho City. After the steep climb, horses would be changed and passengers could enjoy a good meal. The stop boasted four private rooms and a communal bunk area on the second floor

On the west slope of Timber Butte, Maria and I met a Native American fellow who introduced himself as Short Round. When I asked why people called him Short Round, his reply was simply, "None of your business."

After a short visit, he warmed up and we got to be buddies. He showed Maria and me around Timber Butte and, surprisingly, invited us to his home. "I'm gonna show ya somethin' yain't gonna believe," he said.

We wound our way so far into the backlands on a long, dusty road that I started having my doubts about our new friend, wondering why he would lead us so far off the beaten path. But just as I was about ready to give up the trek, we arrived at his home. I'm glad I stuck with it. He showed us an amazing treasure, a wonderful old granary, intact but unused.

Images from the Sweet Idaho Project

The next issue of **Wander Northwest** features the "Bear Lake Project" and the "Silent City Project." I'll show off the work of some very talented people and offer a look at one of the most amazing treasures I have ever come across, an authentic, Oregon Trail blacksmith/wheelwright shop. The shop looks like someone locked the doors 100 years ago and just walked away.

Future Publications

Bear Lake Project

Four Rivers Project

Owyhee Project

The Silent City Project

Joseph's Prairie Project

www.facebook.com/wandernorthwest

Along with my contact information, Facebook also has many works of representational art and short stories that won't be offered in the publications. I add new images and stories as often as life allows and I promise you'll enjoy every one.

My thanks to all of the artists who allowed me to use there work in illustrating this publication.
Jerry Wilda: A mighty man of GOD and my friend.

Wildlife
Illustrator
for Idaho
Fish & Game
Department

Original art work of Jerry Wilda, Illustrator for Idaho Fish & Game Department

Jerry's works are available at www.wandernorthwest.com

Tami Peck is a direct descendent of the settling family of Idaho's Camas Prairie. She is Camas County's' resident historian and curator for the local museum.

http://www.fairfieldidaho.net/community/history

David Eveningthunder spent his early childhood on the Shoshone-Bannock trust lands of Fort Hall. the heart of David's work is to pay tribute to the   contemporary Native American Dancers who help keep the traditions of his ancestors alive.

www.artnatam.com/evnthun/index.html

Jay is sure to become an important Idaho artist. The son of a working cowboy, Jay grew up on ranches throughout the Northwest and was inspired by the beauty and rich history of the American west.

www.jayandersonart.com

Don't forget about Maria and me.

www.facebook.com/wandernorthwest
wandernorthwest@gmail.com

Made in United States
Troutdale, OR
02/20/2024

17812684R00038